aquarium

set up and maintenance
of the perfect aquarium

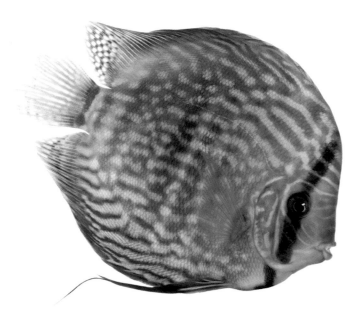

Written by
Lance Jepson MA VetMB CBiol MSB MRCVS

aquarium

set up and maintenance
of the perfect aquarium

Written by
Lance Jepson MA VetMB CBiol MSB MRCVS

Magnet & Steel Ltd

www.magnetsteel.com

Every reasonable care has been taken in the compilation of this publication. The Publisher and Author cannot accept liability for any loss, damage, injury or death resulting from the keeping of fish by user(s) of this publication, or from the use of any materials, equipment, methods or information recommended in this publication or from any errors or omissions that may be found in the text of this publication or that may occur at a future date, except as expressly provided by law.

No animals were harmed in the making of this book.

The 'he' pronoun is used throughout this book instead of the rather impersonal 'it', however no gender bias is intended.

Printed and bound in South Korea.

ISBN: 978-1-907337-18-5
ISBN: 1-907337-18-0

Contents

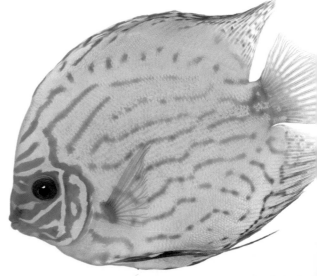

The aquarium

Keeping an aquarium, or fish tank, can be a fascinating pastime. Watching healthy fish going about their business in their apparently weightless world is a relaxing experience, and following their day-to-day lives can be more addictive than television soap operas.

When it is done properly, fish-keeping also teaches you something that no TV programme can – hands-on practical skills of animal care, an empathy for animal-life and a direct awareness of other lands and ecosystems way beyond our actual experience. You can literally bring a piece of the mighty Amazon River into your own living room.

Fish are living creatures and when we decide to set-up and keep an aquarium, we must repay their beauty and their fascinating behaviours with care and respect. This book will show you how.

Pictured:
A mixed shoal of Rainbowfish is a joy to behold, for both young and old.

Your new aquarium

Establishing a successful aquarium can be likened to a marathon rather than a sprint. A truly successful aquarium takes time to establish because it is a living ecosystem – a complex environment that relies heavily upon two types of living organisms for its continued health.

One group is the bacterial colonies that we need to establish in the filtration systems to remove biological fish waste, and the other is YOU. As the owner, you need to feed, check temperatures, service equipment and undertake regular partial water changes to keep the aquarium and its inhabitants in tip-top condition.

Deciding on your aquarium

Most people starting this hobby will have an idea in their mind about what kind of aquarium they want to achieve, Typically these are:

- **Tropical community.**

- **Temperate community.** Many 'tropical' fish regularly available are actually happier at room temperatures between around 16 to 22°C (61–72°F). Such fish often originate from countries either side of the Tropics of Cancer and Capricorn, or are found at higher elevations, where temperatures are cooler.

Pictured:
A discus (Symphysodon sp) is a stunning fish for a single species aquarium.

- **Single or limited species.** This can be for a single individual fish to be kept as a pet, or as a shoal or breeding group. This can take a great deal of self-restraint but can be very rewarding!

- **Nano-aquaria.** At their best these can be small, stylish focal points that have integral filtration and lighting units. Their water volume is only a few litres, which means that temperature and water quality can be unstable and changes rapid. However, if aquascaped appropriately and stocked with small fish or invertebrates, they can be fascinating tabletop works of art.

- **Goldfish**. Take the time to decide what it is that you want from an aquarium. Most people opt for a community aquarium of tropical freshwater fish. This gives the widest choice possible of potential species, and I would consider around 120 litres (26 gal; 31 US gal) as a minimum volume for such an aquarium. If you want a species aquarium (and these can look stunning) or a tank for a single individual, the size can be tailored to your needs. Goldfish are covered in another volume in this series.

Pictured:
A group of goldfish requires a large and well-maintained aquarium and the payoff? – an eye catching display!

Types of aquarium

As a general rule, the bigger the aquarium the better. Larger water volumes have more stable water temperatures and water quality, and you can put more fish in them! However, large aquaria are more expensive and can be extremely heavy. Water is very heavy, and by the time gravel, rockwork and other ornaments are factored in, a 120 litre aquarium could easily weigh some 130 kg (286 lb).

The aquaria pictured are suitable for 1 or 2 small goldfish, or a paradise fish.

Therefore check that the furniture an aquarium is to be located on is sufficiently sturdy. For larger fish tanks the flooring should be checked to ensure that it can bear the weight. Ideally, always place your aquarium on a commercially-made aquarium stand. These are designed to accommodate the weight of the aquarium and usually have a matching trim or effect to enhance the appearance of the tank.

Another consideration is whether the aquarium is glass or acrylic. Glass tanks are heavier, scratch resistant and usually rectangular in shape. Acrylic aquaria can be moulded to a variety of shapes, including spheres. They are lighter, but are more susceptible to being scratched. This is especially important when cleaning algae off the inside surfaces as some cleaners will scour a fine mesh of tiny abrasions that can reduce transparency.

The different types of aquaria available offer a variety of possible fish-keeping experiences. For example:

Standard rectangular aquaria

These are the best all-round aquaria that offer flexibility in sizes available, which species that can be kept housed in them, plus varied lighting and filtration options. Many branded aquaria have integral lighting and filtration systems that are either hidden from view or tooled for a stylish appearance. Surface area is vital, as this is where oxygenation of the water occurs.

A tall aquarium will have a smaller surface area than a shallower tank of the same dimensions, and therefore holds less fish.

Nano-aquaria

These are small aquaria and which hold a very small volume of water. The best of these have built in filtration units, and some have integral lighting units.

Acrylic bowls with integral filtration units

These are stylish and modern looking. The curved surfaces can alter the viewing experience and cleaning can be tricky, but there is a range of products designed to help with the maintenance of such bowls. The water volume can be small compared to traditional aquaria.

'Themed' aquaria

These aquaria are often marketed as 'entry level' set-ups and are usually targeted towards children. Typically they are small acrylic aquaria that are brightly coloured and are often themed with children-related subjects, such as cartoon characters. Such aquaria have the same intrinsic problems as nano-aquaria and, even though they are usually supplied with small power-filters, the maintenance of suitable water conditions can be challenging even in experienced hands. These aquaria are not ideal for the long-term care of goldfish; a single male Paradise fish (Macropodus opercularis) makes a much more suitable pet. The Paradise fish is happy at room temperatures and is a fish that can be trained to jump for its food!

Checklist

Once you have chosen your aquarium, there is a basic checklist of items that you need to buy. The list is:

[✓] Pet Friendly: Aquarium Book

[ ] Aquarium

[ ] Substrate

[ ] Background

[ ] Filter

[ ] Air pump, air tubing and air stone (optional)

[ ] Heater (for tropical aquaria)

[ ] Filter maturation product

[ ] Lighting

[ ] Timer

[ ] Water conditioner

[ ] Bucket (preferably food grade) for water changes

[ ] Flexible tubing for siphoning

[ ] Thermometer

[ ] Net

[ ] Water testing equipment

[ ] Ornamentation

[ ] Fish food

[ ] A cheap diary

Substrate

The substrate is what you place on the bottom of the aquarium. Typically this is a gravel of some description, but silver (or play) sand is also suitable. Do not use builders' sand, as this can be quite sharp or beach sand because of the high salt content. Coral sand is really only suitable for marine aquaria.

The substrate serves several functions. It helps the fish to orientate correctly – fish in unfurnished aquaria will often swim at odd angles. It also provides something for fish such as corydoras catfish to grub around in. What you choose for a substrate is entirely up to you, and most aquatic retail outlets will stock a range of fish-safe substrates. If you want a natural appearance to your aquarium, consider using normal pea gravel which, with its muted tones and rounded shapes, will give a neutral backdrop to your fish. Alternatively, you can choose gravel stained with bright colours – often garishly so. Generally fish look better against black, dark or natural tones as this encourages them to display their brightest colours. The lighter the substrate colour the paler the fish will become as it attempts to blend in.

Fish look better against the more muted tones of natural gravel opposite, but if you want red, the choice is yours!

|Background

It is usually best to use a background. Again, as with substrates, it helps the fish to orientate and produces a backdrop against which your aquascaping and your fish can be viewed. It will also hide unsightly wires and plumbing behind the back glass. As with substrates, what you choose is entirely up to you. A plain black background often works best; blue can work, but does not look as natural with freshwater aquaria as it does with marine.

Photographic backgrounds are also available which depict underwater scenes – usually of plants and rocks, but occasionally of ruined cities or even cartoon-like fish or similar. The main downside with scenic backgrounds is that, mounted on the back as they usually are, any algae, scratches or other blemishes present on the back glass pane will immediate destroy any illusion or perspective of depth.

As an alternative there are moulded backgrounds that can be attached to the inside of the aquarium – these usually depict realistic rock and root formations – and can provide a dramatic backdrop to your aquascaping.

A variety of photographic backgrounds are available to suit all tastes.

|Heater

If you are planning to keep tropical fish, you will need an aquarium heater. These are thermostatically controlled and are usually pre-set to around 25°C(77°F), but can be altered if necessary.

If you are keeping large, robust fish such as Central American cichlids or Oscars (Astronotus occellatus) then a heater guard is necessary. Guidance is usually given on the package as what size (wattage) heater you will need for a given volume aquarium. For larger aquaria there is some merit in installing two heaters of a smaller wattage. If one heater fails then the other should at least stop the water temperature from dropping too low; also if the thermostat should stick on one (a rare event) then this rogue heater is unlikely to cook your fish.

You will also need a thermometer to check that your heater is functioning properly. There are usually three types available:

Select your heater according to your aquarium volume.

- Glass ones containing dyed alcohol, suspended from a suction cup on the inside.

- Colourometric LCD thermometers that are stuck permanently in one place on the outside of the aquarium.

- Digital thermometers that are positioned inside the aquarium or outside with a probe placed into the water.

|Lighting

Many branded complete aquaria come with lighting units already installed. Usually these lights are fluorescent tubes that can be either normal T-8s or the brighter, more energy efficient T-5s. LED lights are very economical on power and have much longer life-spans than fluorescent tubes.

LED lights are very economical too and have much longer life-spans than fluorescent tubes. There are some novelty LED lights in different colours that can be used submerged. If you choose to use these to make an underwater lighting display, please remember that fish do not have eyelids and may be stressed by lights shining directly into their eyes, rather than from above as would be the case in nature.

Fish need a period of darkness too so aim to have the lights on for no more than twelve to fourteen hours per day. Placing the lighting on a timer is ideal as this keeps the day-night cycle constant.

Avoid placing your aquarium in direct sunlight. This can cause excessive algal growth in the aquarium and pronounced temperature swings.

A range of lighting is available for aquaria.

Filters & filtration

You cannot keep fish healthily without good water quality, and you cannot keep your water quality good without filtration. Your filter, and how you look after it, is the cornerstone to your success or failure. It is the main life-support mechanism in your fish tank, functioning as it does as a mini-sewerage plant by facilitating the nitrogen cycle (see later).

Filtration can be divided into three main types, and most modern filters contain compartments or products that undertake each of these. The three categories are:

1. Physical filtration

Physical filtration usually involves drawing water through a fine meshed synthetic polymer substance or 'filter wool' that traps any suspended particles such as faeces or plant debris. This will visually clean the water.

2. Biological filtration

Fortunately, all the beneficial filter bacteria important in the nitrogen cycle like the same conditions – plenty of food, plenty of oxygen, tropical temperatures and a suitable place to live. By using certain materials as substrates such as highly porous minerals, ceramics or sponges - which have a huge surface area relative to their volume - and placing these in a good water flow we can provide the optimum conditions for these bacterial friends. Usually the biological section of a filter is placed between the filter wool to strip out any particles that could clog the biological substrate and impede water flow and the chemical filtration which could strip out compounds needed by the bacteria.

The initial establishment of populations of these bacteria sufficient to support a healthy fish community is often referred to as cycling or maturing your aquarium. This is dealt with later.

3. Chemical filtration

At one time the only real chemical filtration available to fish keepers was activated charcoal. This has special properties that help it absorb a wide variety of dissolved compounds – good and bad – from the water. Activated charcoal can remove the organic products that naturally dye aged water a yellowish colour and so helps to improve clarity. Activated charcoal is now available coated on to sponges and made suitable for insertion into internal power-filters.

1. Aqua Carbon

2. Filter Wool

Other forms of chemical filtration have become available recently, including products that will remove dissolved phosphates and even nitrates, both of which can be a cause of nuisance algae.

3. Nitrex

4. Bio-media

Pictured:
Corydoras sterbai

What fish-keepers need to know about water

Aquarists like to keep fish. Fish live in water, so aquarists need to know about water. Obvious isn't it? Think of it as a tool of the trade, but before you go out and spend money on equipment and fish, you need to do a bit of background research.

Pictured:
Success with
modern Discus
hybrids, available in
innumerable varieties,
depends ultimately on
water quality.

Now let's get the first misconception out of the way - clear water is not always good water. Clear water can be good water, but so can pea-soup green water packed with suspended algae. Clear water can be bad water if it has high levels of ammonia in it. You just cannot tell by looking. It is the quality of the water that counts and much of the expense and paraphernalia involved with fish-keeping is concerned with keeping this quality optimal.

To keep a tropical freshwater aquarium looking its best you need to know about temperature, pH, hardness, ammonia, nitrites, nitrates, oxygen, carbon dioxide and chlorine. Fortunately you don't need a PhD in Chemistry to understand these.

Pictured:
Platies (Xiphophorus
maculatus) are hardy
and justifiably popular
aquarium fish.

Temperature

Fish cannot produce their own body heat and if they did most of it would be immediately lost to the surrounding water. Fish are suited to the conditions in which they evolved and have little ability to adapt. For example, Siamese fighting fish (Betta splendens) originate from Southeast Asia, including Thailand, inhabiting shallow pools and paddy fields, where temperatures can soar.

It is not surprising that they are happiest between 25 - 30°C (77 - 86°F). The closely-related Paradise fish is found in more northerly countries such as southern China and Taiwan, and so is happier at more temperate 18 - 22°C (64 - 71°F). Keeping Paradise fish in tropical aquaria often enhances their aggression, because they are at the top end of their temperature range, at levels that stimulates breeding and therefore territoriality. Keep a fish too cold and its ability to digest food, fend off infection or even just live will be severely affected.

Points to remember :

- Research the temperature needs of your fish. They may not be able to adapt to cooler or warmer temperatures.

- Ammonia is more toxic at higher temperatures.

- At very high or low temperatures biological filtration may not work properly.

- Warmer water holds less oxygen.

- Temperature related water quality issues are ammonia, nitrite and oxygen.

pH

The pH of a sample of water is a measure of how acidic or alkaline it is. It is measured along a scale of 1.0 (most acidic) to 14.0 (most alkaline) with pure water occupying a neutral 7.0. Just like temperatures, the pH needs of fish reflect their waters of origin. For example, Rift Lake fish such as Malawi cichlids need a higher pH of around 8.0 to 8.1 while some Amazonian fish such as Discus (Symphysodon spp) need low pH water of between 6.0 to 7.0. In the wild, pH extremes of 5.5 or less can be encountered.

Points to remember :

- Most ornamental fish available are adapted to a pH between 6.5 and 7.5.

- A change of 1 unit on the pH scale is actually a 10 fold change in the acidity of the water. Therefore, a fish transferred from water of pH 7.0 to pH 6.0 experiences a ten fold fall in acidity. You should always make changes gradually to accommodate this.

- Ammonia becomes more toxic at a higher pH.

- It is normal for the pH in aquaria to fall over time. Correct stocking levels, filter maintenance and water changes will reduce this effect and most fish will tolerate this gradual reduction well. However, you should be very careful if tempted to use pH adjusters – as their effect is temporary and pH falls are best addressed by looking at what the underlying problems are.

- pH related water quality issues are carbonate hardness, ammonia, nitrite and carbon dioxide. See also Plants.

|Hardness

Water hardness is a measure of the total mineral salt content of water. If a sample of water has a very high level it is classed as hard, while soft water has little dissolved mineral content.

Just to make life slightly more complex, hardness consists of two parts – General Hardness (or GH) and the Carbonate (or temporary) Hardness (KH).

A range of minerals contribute to water hardness, but the one found in greatest concentrations is calcium carbonate. Because of this, hardness usually refers to the calcium carbonate concentration, and is expressed as milligrams of calcium carbonate per litre of water (mg/l $CaCO_3$).

For general community aquaria, hardness is rarely an issue. Rift Lake cichlids such as the Malawi cichlids require hard water, like their native lakes. Many community tropical fish originate in areas of soft water, but many of them have been bred in captivity for so many generations that they are able to thrive in a wide variety of water hardness.

As a general guide, soft water is 0 – 100 mg/l $CaCO_3$ (0 – 5.5 dH); above this would be classed as hard, with very hard water at 300+ mg/l $CaCO_3$ (18+ dH).

Carbonate Hardness (KH)

Carbonate Hardness is a measure of the bicarbonate levels in the water. If you boil hard water (which therefore has high carbonate hardness) the bicarbonate turns to carbonate. This is why it is called carbonate hardness; why it is also called temporary hardness and why you get lime-scale inside your kettle. KH is important because bicarbonate acts as a pH buffer, preventing or reducing pronounced pH swings. In well-stocked aquaria there is a tendency for the pH to gradually fall. This trend is opposed by the carbonate hardness. Once all of the bicarbonate is used up by this buffering action, a significant and dangerous drop in pH can occur. That is why we need to know about carbonate hardness.

Sources of carbonate hardness include regular water changes, calcium-based substrates and rocks, plus commercially available buffering solutions. Carbonate hardness affects pH.

Ammonia, nitrite & nitrate

Now we are getting to the core of good fish-keeping. Ammonia, nitrite and nitrate are intricately linked with the nitrogen cycle.

Ammonia

Fish produce ammonia as part of their waste. This is excreted in urine and through the gills. Other sources of ammonia are decaying materials such as dead fish or uneaten food. Ammonia is present in two forms when dissolved in water – a relatively non-toxic ammonium form (NH_4+) and a much more toxic ammonia (NH_3). The proportion of ammonium NH_4+ to ammonia NH_3 is dependent upon water temperature and pH. The higher both of these are, the more toxic NH_3 will be present.

Pictured:
Dwarf cichlids such as the Cockatoo Dwarf cichlids (Apistogramma cacatuoides) are very susceptible to raised dissolved ammonia levels.

Points to remember about ammonia :

- Ammonia is removed primarily by the action of Ammonia Oxidizing Bacteria (AOB) present in your filters, which convert it to nitrite. In an emergency it can be removed by adding ammonia binding solutions (which actually covert the toxic NH_3 to non-toxic forms) or absorbing compounds such as zeolite, and can be reduced by partial water changes.

- Persistent ammonia readings in an established aquarium suggest over-feeding, over stocking or inadequate or faulty filtration.

- Sudden pH crashes may kill the AOB, causing a spike in ammonia levels.

- Ammonia related water quality issues are temperature, pH, and nitrite.

Pictured:
A shoal of neon tetras
(Paracheirodon innesi)
in a planted aquarium.

Nitrite

Ammonia is converted to nitrite by beneficial bacteria as part of the nitrogen cycle (see later). Nitrite is much less toxic than ammonia, but is still very dangerous to your fish. Nitrite Oxidizing Bacteria (NOB) in your filter removes any nitrite present, converting it into nitrate.

Points to remember about nitrite:

- Persistent nitrite readings are possibly a consequence of inadequate or faulty filtration.

- Low temperatures and very high ammonia concentrations mean the NOB in the filter is not working properly.

- Nitrite levels can be reduced by partial water changes. The effects can be ameliorated by the addition of aquarium salt at a rate of 30 g per 10 litres. Do not use table or rock salt as these can be toxic to fish; Even aquarium salt can be toxic to plants and some fish.

- Nitrite related water quality issues are caused by ammonia and temperature.

Nitrate

Nitrate is produced by the action of NOB on nitrite. For most fish it is relatively non-toxic, but some are more sensitive to it than others; high levels can stress the fish, making them more susceptible to disease. Some invertebrates, such as shrimps, can have moulting difficulties if exposed to high nitrate concentrations.

- Nitrate related water quality issues are caused by ammonia and nitrite. Otherwise see Nitrogen Cycle next.

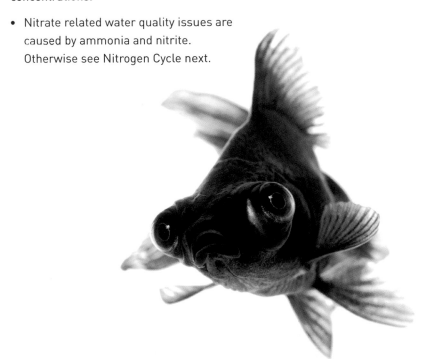

Nitrogen cycle

The constant removal of ammonia and nitrite from your aquarium water by utilising AOB and NOB bacteria is known as biological filtration. The reactions involved form part of the Nitrogen Cycle, and as a fish-keeper you should be familiar with how this works. As outlined previously, the problem with ammonia is that it is very toxic to fish. In the wild, fish are usually found in such large volumes of water that this ammonia is immediately diluted, but in the confines of your aquarium this does not happen. This is why we need biological filtration.

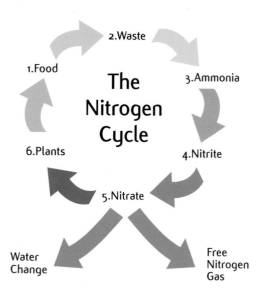

Biological filters provide a suitable environment for the beneficial bacteria that are known collectively as Nitrosomonas (although these Ammonia Oxidizing Bacteria (AOB) are actually Nitrosospira, Nitrosococcus, and Nitrosolobus species) to grow. These AOB feed on dissolved ammonia and convert it into a less toxic compound, nitrite.

Nitrite is still toxic, but another group of bacteria come to the rescue. Collectively referred to as Nitrobacter, these Nitrite-Oxidizing Bacteria (NOB) are usually Nitrospira, Nitrospina, and Nitrococcus. These NOBs then convert any nitrite into nitrate.

Nitrate is considerably less toxic than nitrite and many fish can tolerate high levels, although invertebrates such as shrimps may be less forgiving.

Nitrate is a problem however. In an idealised nitrogen cycle, nitrate would:

1. Be absorbed by plants as food, converted into plant tissue, which, if then eaten by a fish, would complete the nitrogen cycle.

2. Be broken down by bacterial degradation in areas of low oxygen (anaerobic) into free nitrogen gas (denitrification)

3. Be converted back to ammonia (again completing the cycle).

The problem is that this does not happen in most aquaria, and if we do nothing nitrate levels can become extremely high over time. This can usually be traced to:

- High stocking levels causing the production of significant levels of nitrate.

- There being are insufficient live and healthy plants relative to the fish population to utilise much of the nitrate produced.

- No anaerobic areas that allow for denitrification to occur are present. In marine aquaria the utilisation of deep sand beds and plenums are often recommended to achieve this.

In these situations nitrates are controlled either by removal and dilution through partial water changes (although you must make sure that the nitrate levels in your tap water or other water source are lower than in your aquarium) or by using nitrate-removing chemical filtration products.

Oxygen

Fish rely on oxygen dissolved in their surrounding water to breathe. Water has less oxygen than air, and warm water holds less oxygen than cold water. Almost all of the oxygen in a body of water gets there by dissolving into it at the surface. The more agitated the surface, the more oxygen can dissolve. This is why filter outlets placed level with the surface, or spray bars just above it, are so popular. They disturb the surface and enhance oxygenation. Even air stones, air curtains and air-powered ornaments work this way, by bringing less oxygenated water from lower in the aquarium up to the surface. Bubbles also create new surface when they burst at the top, but provide hardly any direct oxygenation at typical aquarium depths.

Pictured:
In a well-stocked aquarium, a bubbling air stone creates a focal point as well as much needed water circulation.

Always make sure that the water surface is rippling or in motion. Powerheads and internal filters placed well below the surface will circulate water, but, if the surface is still, oxygen levels can become dangerously low. Fish that are suffering from oxygen starvation will gasp at the surface. Remember that it is not just your fish that need oxygen – your plants and filter bacteria need it too.

Carbon dioxide

Carbon dioxide is a bi-product of normal respiration. In the aquarium it is produced by your fish, plants and largely by your filter bacteria. It is acidic and high levels can cause a fall in pH, but luckily it comes out of solution and into the air at the surface very easily, so normal water circulation will prevent problems.

Chlorine

Many water companies add chlori or chloramine, to their water supplie to reduce bacterial levels. These are toxic to fish so whenever you do a water change you should use a proprietary dechlorinator.

Pictured:
Large fish such as this black angelfish (Pterophyllum scalare) are more susceptible to low dissolved oxygen levels.

Recommended water quality parameters for community aquaria of various types

Parameter	Typical community aquarium	Rift lake aquarium (lake malawi/ tanganyika)	Temperate community aquarium
Temperature °C	22 - 26	22 - 26	18 - 22
pH	6.8 - 7.5	8.0 - 8.3	6.8 - 7.5
General hardness (GH)(mg $CaCO_3$)	60 - 200	200 +	60 - 200
Carbonate hardness (KH) (mg $CaCO_3$)	50 - 100	>80	50 - 100
Conductivity (μs/cm)	500 - 800	800+	500 - 800
Ammonia (total) (mg/l)		< 0.02 mg/l but the high pH requires ammonia should be 0.0 mg/l	< 0.02
Nitrite (mg/l)	< 0.02	< 0.02	< 0.02
Nitrate (mg/l)	<40 mg above ambient tap water levels	<40 mg above ambient tap water levels	<40 mg above ambient tap water levels
Chlorine (mg/l)	<0.002	<0.002	<0.002

Filters

Filters come in a variety of models. Most are driven by an electric impeller in the form of a powerhead. The smallest filters are usually internal filters and can consist of little more than a sponge cartridge through which water is drawn by a small powerhead. Larger internal filters are often designed to hold materials that provide physical, biological and chemical filtration, with companies often providing bespoke products to suit their range of filters. Some branded aquaria have integral filtration units that are tucked unobtrusively in one back corner.

External filters follow the same general principle as internal ones, but because they are not constrained by aquarium size or viewing aesthetics, they can be quite large and contain several compartments that can be used for different types of filter media.

Pictured:
Internal filters
(foreground) are
typically smaller than
external filters (rear).

External filters are usually housed beneath the aquarium, often in tailor-made cupboards built into the design of the stand. Water is drawn down and pumped back into the aquarium via flexible tubing looped over the back. Their large size and ease of access for maintenance are major advantages over internal filters.

Sponge filters are sometimes used for smaller aquaria, or breeding and rearing tanks. These are usually powered by air delivered by a pump rather than a powerhead. This gives a gentler flow that is safer for young fish and fry.

Undergravel filters have largely fallen out of favour now. They are simple in structure and concept – an undergravel filter consists of a perforated plastic plate with one or two uplift tubes. It is installed during the set-up of the aquarium, beneath a layer of gravel some 5 cm (2 inches) deep. Air stones or powerheads are used to pull water along the uplifts, which has the effect of drawing water down through the gravel. The gravel acts as both a physical filter and a biological medium. Undergravel filters are extremely effective biological filters, but need regular stirring and siphoning off of debris from within the gravel layers to prevent eventual clogging.

Excessive debris retention or disturbance by digging fish such as cichlids can cause channelling or short-circuiting of water flows, which can dramatically reduce the functioning of the filter bed. Many plants do not seem to grow well in aquaria with undergravel filters. In an aquarium with low stocking densities and small, non-disruptive fish they can still have a place.

Biological filter media will, over time, become progressively clogged with bacteria and associated debris, and so will need cleaning. But true cleaning, even under ordinary tap water, will remove the AOB and the NOB that you have worked so hard to establish. The best method is to rinse it in discarded aquarium water at the time of a water change, so that the bacteria left on the filter material will not be harmed. In larger aquaria two filters can be used. Aside from doubling your filter capacity, it also means that you can clean them alternately, so that at any given time one filter is not disturbed.

|Aeration

Pictured:
Modern air pumps
are much quieter
than older models.
Air curtains can
produce dramatic
effects with enhanced
circulation.

For many budding aquarists, the archetypal aquarium will have a stream of bubbles rising to the surface somewhere. Air stones are an excellent way of giving good water circulation, although as we have mentioned the bubbles actually do little oxygenation themselves.

Once air pumps were essential and all filters were air-powered, but now much of the equipment is run with electric motors. However, air stones can still have their place. They can enhance oxygenation by surface disruption and circulation, add to an aesthetic effect and are useful alongside smaller power foam filters that are used in fry-rearing tanks, where a vigorous current is not needed.

|Test kits

Test kits are vital pieces of equipment. Without them you have no idea of what is really happening in your aquarium. Most of the commonly available test kits are colourimetric – you interpret the result by reading a colour change off against a chart provided. Types of testing kit are:

Dip strips

These are strips of card with small squares that house the chemistry. They are dipped into your aquarium water and the results read off against a chart at specific time intervals. Often several tests are incorporated on to one strip.

Liquid tests

Specific chemicals are added to a standard volume of water, and any colour change is noted.

Tablet tests

As for liquid tests, but the active ingredients are in tablet form that need dissolving or crushing.

Electronic test kits

These are usually very accurate, if expensive.

A whole range of parameters can be tested, but the most important are ammonia, nitrite and nitrate. Don't forget temperature as well!

Pictured:
A colour wheel to
interpret pH tests.

Aquascaping

A display aquarium can be thought of as a living work of art, and like any artwork, what you think is attractive is very subjective. Some aquarists look to mimic actual habitat and will research it - often with the use of the Internet - whilst others will attempt artistic interpretations of landscape vistas by playing with scale, creating mountains from rocks and forests of dwarf plants. Other aquarists prefer bubbling divers, small castles and sunken galleons. The truth is, providing it does not harm the fish, anything goes.

If we consider your aquarium as a canvas, looked at from the front, we can borrow some basic picture composition rules for use in aquascaping to create an attractive aquarium. If this seems a bit over the top, remember that a well-maintained aquarium could be the focal point of the room.

Pictured:
With a little planning, your aquarium can be a stunning, artistic mirror of nature.

Points to consider:

Asymmetry

Always try to avoid designing your aquarium layout too symmetrically. Such an aquarium loses its illusion of nature and much of its spontaneity.

The rule of thirds

Look at the front of your aquarium. Mentally (or on a piece of paper) draw two pairs of lines that will divide your aquarium into three sections vertically and three horizontally. You should aim to place your main objects of interest either along these lines, or where these lines cross. If you have a particular object, such as a plant, rock or ornament that you wish to use as a focal point, place it as best you can where two of these lines intersect.

Pictured:
Plants and rocks can be
used as focal points.

The rule of odds

The human brain automatically tries to make sense of any scene that it beholds, and one thing it does is to look for symmetry. This it done by attempting to pair everything up. If you have even numbers of anything – plants, rocks or bubbling divers – your brain will pair these up and this will lessen the impact of your display. Therefore, try to keep odd numbers of plants, rocks and aquarium ornaments, so that the brain cannot form pairs, which in turn means that a more haphazard, and more naturalistic, effect is achieved.

Bigger things go to the back

Generally taller plants and bogwood are placed towards the back, whilst smaller objects or plant life are brought to the front. This helps to give an illusion of depth.

Rocks strata

Rocks strata in nature tend to run in the same direction, so if you are trying to reproduce a rock formation effect, try to use similar-looking rocks and have them all roughly arranged at a similar angle. Only use rocks bought as safe for use in aquaria. Rocks from unknown sources may contain toxic minerals.

Substrate size

For natural-looking aquaria use different size substrates at different points in the aquarium. For example, use silver sand grading to gravel with some larger pebbles and rocks scattered on to it to resemble a river bed. Make sure that there is not too much variation in the colours or tones.

Proportion

Try to keep everything in proportion. If you are trying to suggest a mountain range with a series of large rocks, stock with small fish. Big fish with small castles just look wrong!

Pictured:
Artificial rocks and caves can be just as good as the real thing – just ask this Golden gourami (Trichogaster trichopterus).

Bogwood

This and similar woods can add a strong natural element to an aquarium, often helping to form the basic skeleton of your submerged work of art. Wooden roots and branches add visual interest, provide scaffolding for plants to grow on, resting-places for certain fish and help define territorial boundaries for others. Bogwood is wood that has been naturally preserved with tannins. If it is dry then it is highly likely to float when placed in water – this is especially true for smaller pieces. Once it becomes waterlogged it will settle, but the tannins it contains will leach out into the water for quite a while. This is normal and should not be a cause for concern as many of the fish we keep are native to tannin-stained waters. Activated carbon and partial water changes will progressively remove the tannins. If you are really organised you can place any new pieces of bogwood into a bucket of water a week or so before you set up your aquarium, so that it becomes waterlogged. Otherwise, floating pieces of bogwood can be tied down to rocks or pieces of slate using cotton or aquarium-safe epoxy putty used by modellers. Do not use driftwood from the beach as this will be saturated with salt that is potentially poisonous to your freshwater fish. Nor should you use fresh wood, as this may contain harmful substances in the sap. Feel free to experiment. After all, an aquarium is a personal thing.

Pictured:
Bogwood is used as a resting perch for a variety of fish, including this Peckotlia catfish.

Aquarium plants

Plants are thought to have several beneficial uses, including aesthetic appearance, providing shelter and food, enhancing the water quality by utilising fish waste products and oxygenating the water. In reality, in the typical home aquarium, only the first two happen.

As for utilising fish waste, not all plants will use nitrate as a food – some will absorb ammonia instead, which can be good or it can interfere with the initial cycling of an aquarium. In heavily-stocked aquaria the nitrate produced may be in excess of what the plants need.

During the day, under sufficient light intensity plants photosynthesise, and as a bi-product of these chemical reactions, release oxygen into the water (sometimes little streams of tiny bubbles can be seen trickling from leaves up towards the surface).

Pictured:
Mixing and matching
different artificial plants
can give a very realistic
display.

Dissolved carbon dioxide is used during photosynthesis and so, as this acidic substance is removed, the pH can rise. During the night photosynthesis stops, but the plants continue to breathe, using up oxygen which means that they compete with the fish and the filter bacteria, and release carbon dioxide which can cause a pH drop.

Another point to be aware of is that many aquarium plants are actually bog plants that are able to live both above and below the water. Such plants often have two types of form – the immerse which grows beneath the surface, and an emerse – which grows above the surface. Some plants, such as Amazon swords (Echinodorus spp) are commercially grown in the emerse state; once placed into your fish tank the old emerse-form leaves will die off and be replaced by flimsier immerse ones.

True, beautiful, take-your-breath-away planted aquaria take a great deal of time and effort to achieve. In these set-ups the plants come first and are provided with lighting of the correct spectrum, fertilizer both in the substrate and dissolved in the water, carbon dioxide supplementation and careful management of dissolved compounds such as phosphate.

Pictured:
To get a planted aquarium this good requires correct lighting, substrate, supplements and time.

Such aquaria also have a relatively reduced load of carefully-selected fish that will not burrow or grub too deep into the substrate, eat or damage the plants, or consume nuisance algae. Some of these aquaria are truly stunning and it is possible to achieve this with research and application. Many plants placed into normal community aquaria will fade and die because they are living organisms too, and just like fish, they have certain requirements. Those I would recommend to cut your aquatic plant teeth on are:

Java fern

Java fern (Microsorium pteropus) this aquatic fern is robust and grows well in low light conditions. It can be trained to cling to rocks and bogwood, and can be bought already attached. Older leaves tend to turn brown and rot. It is slow growing, but extremely hardy, and is generally unpalatable to vegetarian fish. Suitable for tropical and temperate aquaria, it is available in at least two leaf forms.

Java moss

Java Moss (Taxiphylluim barbieri) is usually referred to under its old name of Vesicularia dubyana (which is in reality a different moss - the Singapore moss) and is another plant that does well at low light levels.

Pictured:
Artificial plants removes the need for specialist plant care and can be used with a variety of non-plant friendly fish.

Left to its own devices it will slowly spread into a mass of strands and will harbour all kinds of micro-organisms that your fish will love to graze on. Many fish will spawn on, or in it. Suitable for tropical or temperate aquaria, it can be grown or bought on bogwood or rocks.

Amazon swords

Amazon Swords (Echinodorus spp). There are a variety of Amazon sword species and most are large. Planted singly in smaller aquaria or in groups in larger aquaria, they usually do well under normal aquarium conditions. Expect the upright leaves to die off over a period of several weeks to be replaced by similar, but less rigid, leaves. Amazon Swords are tropical, but will tolerate temperatures to around 18°C.

Vallisneria

Often referred to as simply 'vallis', Vallisneria spiralis has long tape-like leaves that can be well over twelve inches long. Planted in groups, especially towards the back, these vallis clumps will thicken as the parent plants send out runners across the surface of the substrate. It thrives in both tropical and temperate conditions.

Anubias

These African plants have broad flat leaves and are very tolerant of low light levels – in fact, if exposed to too much illumination, they can suffer badly from algal overgrowth. They generally grow very slowly, and, like the Java fern and moss, can be grown on rockwork and bogwood. This is suitable for tropical aquaria only.

Canadian pond weed

Canadian pond weed (Elodea canadensis) Typically sold in bunches, this plant can grow very rapidly and will quickly become quite straggly without appropriate lighting and pruning. The rapid growth does mean that it competes with nuisance algae for available dissolved nutrients, and many fish will eat it, so it can be a good source of greens and fibre. It is suitable for temperate aquaria only. Be careful where you dispose of this plant, as it can quickly become a pest in native waterways - the compost heap is best. This, and the related species E. densa, are illegal in some states of the USA and some Australian territories.

Two of the remaining functions of plants – aesthetics and shelter – can equally be achieved by artificial plants. There are some very realistic plastic, acrylic and silk plants available today. These can be mixed and matched for form, colour, texture and size to give some truly remarkable results. You can even combine them with real plants too. If artificial plants become algae-coated they are easily removed, cleaned off with a mildly abrasive pad, and replaced. They can also be kept with plant-eating fish such as Silver Dollars (Metynnis spp) and will not succumb to the over-eager attentions of sucking catfish.

Plants are often considered an integral part of an aquarium, and it is true that some of the most stunning aquaria are heavily planted, but they are not essential. In fact many fish are found in waters where there are little or no plants.

Pictured:
Veiltail angelfish
against a backdrop
of plants growing on
bogwood. Beautiful.

Setting up your aquarium

This is the beginning of the exciting bit – setting up your aquarium. All the reading and thinking that you have been doing on filtration systems, water quality and what fish you are going to keep is now brought in to play.

The steps to a successful aquarium:

1. Place your aquarium on a dedicated stand or on furniture strong enough to hold the total weight. All-glass aquaria, especially medium to large ones, are best set on a soft, conforming base. This is to even out any minute differences in pressure between the aquarium stand and the glass base that could cause cracks when the tank is filled. Foam bases are available, or as an alternative use polystyrene ceiling tiles cut to size. Avoid direct sunlight.

2. Add any large rocks or other heavy ornaments. They can be placed on small piece of polystyrene tile to spread the weight over the glass bottom thereby avoiding points of pressure. Then add your gravel or other substrate, and bed other ornamentation, such as bogwood, into place. If you are using an under-gravel filter this will need to be positioned first.

3. Begin adding water. Siphon or gently pour water on to a small plate or sheet of paper placed on the gravel, allowing the water to spill over the side in a fashion less likely to disturb your initial aquascaping.

4. The water that you are adding at this stage need not be heated, but should contain a water conditioner to remove any chlorine and heavy metals that may be present in your tap water. Bubbles will form on the sides of the aquarium and on the surfaces within – this is normal. If the aquarium is not too deep – between 30 and 45 cm (12 and 18 inches) – then wait until the aquarium is 80% full before adding any further aquascape elements, as you can best judge what the effect will be in at this point. For a deeper aquarium, wait until it is around one third full. Some people will add live plants at this stage. If you are going to do this, fill with water warmed to the correct temperature, as many plants will not tolerate a cold shock.

5. Once around 80% full, install the heater and internal filters, or the siphons, return pipes and spray bars for external filtration units. Switch on and prime your filters, making sure everything is working well. It is common for air pockets to be present when filters are first run. These can make the filtration units seems noisy and may cause intermittent fine sprays of tiny bubbles into the aquarium. Once these are going steadily you can begin to add the maturation product according to the instructions – you have started cycling your aquarium (see later).

6. Switch on the power to your heaters once the aquarium is full.

7. Place any cover glasses on and put the lid or hood in place.

8. Now leave your aquarium to settle in for a few days. Check the temperature frequently to make sure that it is reaching your desired temperature (or room temperature if you have a temperate aquarium). Live plants benefit from at least five to seven days to start to establish themselves before introducing any fish. If live plants are used, start switching the light on (or put on a timer) as they need to start to photosynthesise.

Pictured:
A slice of the Amazon -
Discus (Symphysodon
sp) combined with
Rummy-nosed tetras
(Hemigrammus
rhodostomus).

Cycling your aquarium

Cycling an aquarium is the process of establishing and maturing the biological filtration necessary for the safe and rapid detoxification of ammonia into nitrate. Failure to cycle your aquarium will result in New Tank Syndrome, and will cause unnecessary suffering to your fish.

New Tank Syndrome happens when fish are added to a new aquarium immediately after it is set up. With no filter maturation products, high numbers of fish and regular feeding, the ammonia levels rapidly rise to 2.0 mg/l and above, causing fatalities in all but the hardiest of fish.

Cycling an aquarium typically takes some three to four weeks, but it can take longer, because each aquarium is different.

Once you are happy that your aquarium is settling down – the temperature is stable and all pumps and filters are working - start adding your maturation product. Such products contain colonies of the beneficial AOB and NOB that you need to seed in your filtration system to make your aquarium suitable for keeping fish in. Bacteria can be added as:

- Commercial products. The bacteria are present either in a liquid suspension, gel or powder

- Seeding from an established filter by transferring some filter material or squeezing some media out into the aquarium or filter.

- Introduction of live plants will bring in some beneficial bacteria.

To establish a population of filter bacteria you need a source of ammonia. Usually this is the fish, but there are fishless methods of cycling an aquarium, using either pure ammonium added directly to the aquarium or allowing something high in protein to rot in your tank – often a piece of prawn is used. These methods, although arguably better from a fish welfare point of view, are less predictable. Most aquarists use a combination of good commercial bacterial supplement, combined with the introduction of small numbers of ammonia tolerant fish.

No fish is immune to ammonia however, and even those suggested should be closely monitored for signs of ill health.

Commonly available species of fish that are suitable for the initial cycling of an aquarium are:

- Danios, especially the Zebra Danio (Danio rerio) and all of its forms, plus the Pearl Danio (D. albolineatus). Both suitable for tropical or temperate aquaria.

- White Cloud Mountain minnows (Tanichthys albonubes). They are suitable for tropical or temperate aquaria.

- Corydoras catfish (Corydoras sp) for tropical aquaria, and the Peppered Catfish Corydoras paleatus (normal and albino) is suitable for temperate aquaria.

- Barbs (Barbus sp). Note that some of these can be quite big and boisterous as adults and should only be bought if you are confident that they will fit within your intended final species grouping.

- Tetras such as the Neon Tetra (Paracheirodon innesi) and Cardinal Tetra (P. axelrodi).

Pictured:
Neon tetras, initially in very small numbers, can be used for cycling a tropical aquarium.

Cycling your aquarium is really where your test kits and cheap diary come in, because you need to keep a record of the different water quality readings over the days to help you judge how your aquarium is maturing. Your essential test kit should cover pH, ammonia, nitrite and temperature.

Method for cycling your aquarium

- Most bacteria supplied in the maturation products are present in a dormant form, and can take between two to six days to become active, therefore once your aquarium has settled down, start adding the maturation product according to the instructions supplied. Usually it is added daily.

- After a few days it will be safe to add some fish. Only buy a small number – around two or three depending upon size. Feed only small amounts several times daily. Check the ammonia level and make a note of it in your diary. This is Day One of Cycling.

- Every day or two check the ammonia level and note it. It should progressively climb and reach a peak around Day 10 to 14. Once the ammonia reaches a level of around 2.0 mg/l, start monitoring your fish very closely. Continue to add maturation product and, if this does not halt the rise, add an 'ammonia-locking' solution.

Pictured:
A fully cycled and
fully stocked tropical
aquarium.

These products convert ammonia into less toxic ammonium – your test kit will measure and read the total ammonia (the sum of NH_3 and NH_4+), the filter bacteria will still be able to work on the ammonium to convert it to nitrite, but it will be less toxic to your fish. The peak ammonia concentration is likely to be high - up to 4.0 or 5.0 mg/l. Once the AOB numbers in your filtration system have multiplied to a level where they can remove all of the ammonia present, you will see a sudden and dramatic fall in ammonia. This can occur literally within 24 hours. It can seem a long time coming, but is exciting when it does and means, you're half way there.

- Around day 5 to 7, start to measure your nitrite levels. Initially this can be done every other day. The same process that the AOB went through, your NOB now have to go through. At this point there will be a huge population of AOB kicking out vast amounts of nitrites for a relatively small population of NOB to deal with. Now the NOB, with all this nitrite available, begins to multiply. This process always seems to take longer than the first part – nitrites typically peak around Day 25 to 35, but even after levels have fallen, there is often nitrite present for several weeks.

- Now nitrates will begin to rise, and their levels are kept in check largely by partial water changes.

- Once the nitrite peak has been and gone, you can stock with more fish. Aim to stock over a period of three to four months or more. Each time you add a new fish, the bacterial populations need to go through the same process of multiplying to meet demand. Therefore, after each addition monitor your ammonium and nitrite levels closely. Demand is relative, however. If you have one fish and add a second identical fish, you have doubled the ammonia load on your filter system. On the other hand if you have ten fish and you add one more identical one, then you have increased the load by about 10% only.

- Technically your aquarium is never completely mature, but your filtration system should be healthy enough to respond quickly to variations in fish load.

- Check your pH at least every 2 to 3 days. The high levels of bacteria that you are encouraging can cause an inadvertent fall in pH.

- Cycling an aquarium can take up to five weeks, because every tank is different. This is not wasted time however, you are preparing the ground for the aquarium that you first visualised in your head or were inspired to replicate. This time will have given you valuable experience looking after those first few fish needed to cycle your aquarium, and will have given you a chance to research species you wish to keep once those nitrite levels fall. There are probably 200 species of fish commonly available in aquatic outlets, that are suitable for inclusion in community aquaria, and even more once you begin to look at specialist set-ups or less common species. Take the time while your aquarium is maturing to read around or talk to assistants in your local pet & aquatics store. Impulse buys often end up as problems.

Pictured:
Take time to build up to
high stocking levels.

Populating your aquarium

Remember that at the beginning of the book we said that setting up an aquarium was a marathon and not a sprint? Well, this is the moment that you have been waiting for – the finishing line is in sight. Your aquarium is cycled and you have a few, small, non-aggressive fish looking very lost in your aquarium. Do you rush out and buy a whole load of fish straight away? As you might have guessed, the answer is no.

Pictured:
A 5 cm Dalmatian molly
(Poecilia hybrid) needs
120 cm² of surface area.

Aside from researching individual fish species, you need to consider how many fish your aquarium can support. As a general rule aim for 2.5 cm (1 inch) of fish to 60 cm² of surface area (do not include the tail fin when measuring). As an example, a standard 60 x 30 x 45 cm aquarium has a surface area of (60 x 30) cm = 1,800 cm² and will therefore hold 30 cm (12 inches) of fish. This is not a hard and fast rule because you should also consider what effect fish size can have on waste production. A 30 cm (12 inches) parrot cichlid (Cichlasoma hybrid) will produce far more ammonia and faecal waste than 15 neon tetras each measuring 2.5 cm (1 inch).

Other factors that affect how many of what type of fish you can keep are:

1. Aquarium size. If your aquarium is 60 cm (24 inches) long then trying to shoehorn a fish that grows to 45 cm (18 inches) into it is unfair and could easily cause welfare problems.

2. Water quality. Filtration systems can be overloaded by excessively high fish populations. Such aquaria have poor water quality with very high nitrate levels and surges of ammonia and nitrite.

3. Low oxygen levels resulting from inadequate circulation can also be a problem. More advanced forms of filtration can potentially push the stocking levels higher, but at the risk of a catastrophe if you suffer a prolonged power cut, for example.

4. Sociability. Some fish are natural loners. They may be territorial either permanently, or just while breeding, and attempt to defend an area of the aquarium – sometimes to the death. Their behaviour in the confines of an aquarium may be different from that in the wild too. Midas cichlids (Amphilophus citrinellum) will shoal in the wild when not spawning; in aquaria it can be difficult to keep individuals together in all but the largest tanks.

5. Do not judge your potential fish numbers by what you see in the aquatic shops. These fish are usually kept in large systems where all of the aquaria are connected, plus there will be a large sump full of high-tech filtration equipment so that in reality these fish are swimming in a huge volume of water.

6. The biological load of invertebrates is considered tiny and any shrimps, snails and so on that you are thinking of stocking can normally be exempt from your calculations, unless their numbers are going to be large.

Pictured:
Goldfish (here a calico ryukin and red and white bubble-eye) are large, messy fish that require a relatively large amount of space.

Other guidelines to consider when choosing fish are:

Less is more

Shoaling fish always look better in larger numbers of the same species. The various tetras for example will school together, but the visual effect of a group of disparate species is less than that of a single one, so if you are planning on buying shoaling fish, always buy at least 5 or more. Fish will shoal or school primarily as an anti-predator behaviour. The more fish you swim with the less chance you have of being selected by a predator. Schooling fish in a group are happy; a single fish is nervous and stressed. Keeping such fish in larger groups makes them more confident, which means that they are more likely to display normal behaviour. Male Black Phantom tetras (Megalamphodus megalopterus) with their jet black sail-like dorsal fins erect, or the vibrant colours of displaying Boesemani rainbowfish (Melanotaenia boesemani) are a sight to behold. Many aquatic outlets will have special offers on shoaling fish with discounts on multiple buys. Stunning aquaria can be achieved by just one or two species of fish.

Rule of odds

This is as true for groups of fish as it is for aquascaping. Where possible, buy odd numbers of shoaling fish, as this looks more natural.

Water column

Some experts recommend selecting fish based on the level in the water column they are likely to swim, in order to give a balanced appearance. But, unless your aquarium is exceptionally deep, this is unlikely to work. Substrate dwellers such as Corydoras catfish will spend most of their time on the bottom, but will swim to the surface to gulp air and to take flake food. Guppies (Poecilia reticulata) are said to inhabit the top layers in nature – which they do, except that the top layer would be the first 30 cm (12 inches) or so of depth, which is the total depth of many aquaria.

Janitors

Do not buy fish solely as janitors. Substrate feeders like Corydoras are sometimes naively sold as 'cleaners', along the lines of 'they feed on any uneaten food.' These fish do comb the bottom looking for food, but they should be fed and cared for as much as any of your fish and will benefit from being kept in social groups (Corydoras are a shoaling species) and fed on sinking pellets and wafers. If they just have to rely on leftovers they can slowly starve to death.

Pictured:
Guppies are best kept
in groups or shoals.

Healthy fish

Only select from obviously healthy fish. Look at the other fish in the same tank. If there are any obviously sick ones do not buy from that tank. For signs of a healthy fish, see Health.

Maintaining your aquarium

Now your aquarium is up and running and your first fish are installed, we move on the important part of keeping them at their best.

Water changes

Regular water changes are an essential part of fish-keeping. They help to reduce the level of organic compounds in the water and replace certain substances that are constantly being removed or reduced from solution. This can include vital trace elements such as iodine. A water change is literally your fishes' breath of fresh air.

It is better to change little and often because then there is less variation in the make-up and quality of the water that the fish inhabit. Aim to change around 10 - 20% of the aquarium volume once weekly. If you are only able to do this less often then you can change more at a time.

Always use a dechlorinator with fresh water. In principle you should make sure that the new water is at the same temperature as the aquarium, but in practice many fish seem to enjoy swimming in a cooler head of water for a few minutes.

Water changes can be used as an opportunity to clean your substrate too. There are siphon tubes connected to wider bore cylinders that can be grubbed around in the gravel. These are known as gravel cleaners. The pieces of gravel are disturbed and rolled around by the current generated by the siphon. Dirt and waste are drawn up and out into your bucket, but in the wider bore tube most of the individual gravel pebbles are too heavy to be sucked all the way up.

Pictured:
Siamese fighting fish
(Betta splendens)
are highly territorial
towards other fighting
fish and similar-looking
species.

|Feeding

Feeding the bulk of tropical and temperate community fish is fairly straightforward. There are several types of foods that are readily available to the aquarist. These are:

Flakes & pellets

Most community fish will take commercial flake or pelleted foods; there are a number of branded varieties available and all are balanced nutritionally. There are also some specialist foods designed for particular groups of fish. For example, several companies offer 'algal wafers' for loricarid catfish and other largely vegetarian fish, while others produce pellets just for Siamese fighting fish (Betta splendens).

Frozen foods

Frozen foods are arguably closer to the natural diet of many of the fish that we keep. The bulk of these frozen foods are invertebrates such as daphnia, bloodworm (Chironomus larvae), mosquito larvae and brine shrimp. Freezing does not destroy certain disease-causing organisms such as mycobacteria, so those which have been gamma-irradiated are safest to feed your fish. Frozen foods can either be thawed out first before being fed, which allows a rapid dispersal of the food within the aquarium, or a frozen block or part block can be just dropped into the water. As it melts pieces of food will fall away, giving a more prolonged, albeit more localised, feeding time.

Pictured:
Frozen fish foods
typically come in
blister packets.

Live foods

Live foods trigger hunting behaviour and can be an invaluable aid for inducing breeding. Brine shrimp, although nutritionally not ideal, is safe for freshwater fish as it is reared in salt water. Freshwater live foods such as daphnia, tubifex worms and bloodworm, may or may not come from cultured sources and so may pose a disease risk.

Feed your fish little and often. Most small fish are micro-predators and would normally feed opportunistically throughout the day on small invertebrates. We should attempt to mimic this by offering food at least twice a day, maybe up to four or five times, but only in small amounts. All food should be consumed around two to five minutes. If there is food left over then you are offering too much, and left over, uneaten food just puts extra strain on your filtration system. Many fish die from the effects that uneaten food has on their water quality where it can cause fatal spikes of ammonia or nitrite.

Pictured:
Live bloodworm is taken
eagerly by most fish.

|Algae

Nuisance algae

Algae in your aquarium is an inevitability. Algal spores are brought in on plants or fish and even blown in on drafts. Usually it is just an aesthetic problem, but occasionally it can get out of hand. A surge of algal growth is normal in newly established aquaria, as nutrient levels can be high and competing live plants are neither established nor numerous enough to grab any dissolved nutrients. In more mature aquaria it is likely to be a management problem reflecting poor conditions. Slime algae (Cyanobacterium, which is actually a type of bacteria) grows in blue-green sheets that expand during the day and contract at night. This is typical of high nutrient, poor water quality conditions.

Physical removal

There are an assortment of mildly abrasive scrubbing pads and magnetic algae cleaners available in shops.

These can be good at removing all or most of the algae off the glass sides of the aquarium; if you have an acrylic aquarium only use those recommended, because some scourers will scratch acrylic. Slime algae can be siphoned off the substrate and ornaments.

Nutrient control

High stocking densities predispose to high algal growth by providing lots of algal food, usually as high nitrate levels (due to over stocking) and high phosphate levels (from fish food). Partial water changes, nitrate and phosphate absorbers and reducing fish numbers will help.

Lighting

The light spectrum or intensity may be wrong for live plants so they grow poorly and are out-competed by algae. Reducing the hours the lights are on, or changing or upgrading your lighting system, will help.

Keeping algae eaters

Only choose these if you want them to be a part of your aquatic community. All of these are animals with specific needs that need to be met – they are not merely small fishy vacuum cleaners. None of these will touch slime algae.

Sucking loach

Sucking loach (Gyrinocheilus aymoneri). Cute when small, they can get large (up to 27 cm [11 inches]) and aggressive too. Probably not recommended long term for a normal community aquarium. Normally coloured in shades of brown, a yellow or gold (xanthic) version is available.

Siamese algae eater

Siamese Algae Eater (Crossocheilus siamensis). Up to 15 cm (6 inches), eats a wide variety of algae but is not very colourful.

Ancistrus sp catfish

These sucking catfish are excellent for algal control. They do not grow too big (between 10 and 15 cm [4 and 6 inches]). They may spawn in a community aquarium, where the male will dig or take over a burrow and tend the eggs and newly-hatched fry. Usually coloured in browns and greys, a stunning golden albino morph is occasionally available, as is a long-finned variety.

Otocinclus sp catfish

A small (5 cm [2 inches]) sucking catfish that prefers to be in shoals and can be delicate until established.

Other sucking catfish

Generally, for algae control, these are a mixed bunch. Some are good but just grow too big, such as the Sailfin plec Glyptoperichthys gibbiceps at 50 – 60 cm (20 – 24 inches), while others are not vegetarian.

Pictured:
Peckoltia sabaji is an omnivore that needs some meaty food in its diet. Grows up to 25 cm (10 inches).

Algae-eating shrimp

Algae-eating shrimp or Amano shrimp (Caridina japonica). This small, semi-transparent shrimp is hardy and suitable for tropical or temperate aquaria. If kept in reasonable numbers they can collectively do a very good job of keeping algae under control.

Chemical control

There are a variety of products that are added to the aquarium to kill algae. I would suggest these as a last resort. They may give a temporary improvement but you are better off trying to address any underlying factors, such as poor water quality.

Pictured:
The Algae-eating
shrimp is ideal for
aquaria with small fish
or nano-aquaria.

Routine aquarium care

Routine care procedures to keep your fish and aquarium in tip-top condition are not particularly onerous and should not take up much time. Guidelines are given for filter-cleaning frequencies with the product instructions, but certain filtration units may have particular maintenance and care schedules suggested by the manufacturers, and these should be followed.

Daily

- Feed your fish

- Check temperature.

- Check filtration systems are working

Weekly

- Undertake water quality tests and log them.

- Partial water change.

- Remove algae from aquarium glass

- Clean sponge filters.

Monthly

- Clean artificial plants and ornaments.

- Clean or change component parts on filters according to manufacturer's instructions.

Six monthly to one year

- Change lighting tubes.

|Health

Signs of health

- Healthy fish will usually be alert and responsive to what is going on around them.

- Their swimming pattern will be normal.

- The fins are usually at half-mast or fully erect.

- The colour will be normal and the skin surfaces unblemished.

- Breathing will be largely unnoticeable, but of slow to moderate rate.

- They will feed readily if offered appropriate food.

Pictured:
Erect fins, bright
colours and balanced
position denote a
healthy Columbian
tetra (Hyphessobrycvon
equadoriensis).

Signs of Illness

- Fish are listless and fins are clamped.

- Some fish may persistently rub or scratch against the substrate or ornaments.

- Breathing may be rapid or exaggerated. Fish may appear to gasp at the surface.

- Swimming movements are abnormal for that species. The fish may be unable to keep an even keel; very weak fish just drift with the current, or become drawn on to or stuck to filter inlets.

- Colours may be dulled; grey patches of mucus may be obvious.

- There may be obvious skin abnormalities including discrete white spots, fluffy cotton-wool like patches and red ulcers.

Pictured:
Avoid mollies with
clamped fins that
shimmy in one spot.

Just like us, fish can suffer from a wide range of ailments. Some of these are easy to sort out, some are difficult and some almost impossible. You will see a range of off-the-shelf treatments available in your local aquatics outlet, but these have varying levels of effectiveness. In some countries such as the USA antibiotics are also available off the shelf. In the UK antibiotic use is tightly controlled and can be dispensed only under veterinary supervision.

These products are generally safe to use in your aquarium. Some species or types of fish can be susceptible to certain ingredients; for example, one should not use products with copper or formalin with scaleless fish such as the Clown Loach (Botia macracantha) and Black Knife Fish (Apteronotus albifrons). Usually there will be a warning on the label for any specific contraindications.

The key to getting the best out of these fish medicines is to be as accurate as possible with your diagnosis, but it is a truism that common things occur commonly. Some of the frequently encountered problems are listed. In the event of a disease outbreak always check your water quality, because this is often the source of the problem, and strive to maintain optimum conditions to give your fish their best chance of recovery.

White spot

White spot is caused by a single-celled parasite called Ichthyophthirius multifilis. This protozoan parasite burrows into the skin where it grows, forming the characteristic white spot. It then drops off the fish, falls on to the substrate and forms a protective cyst. Whilst in this encysted stage the parasite divides into up to 200 new, free swimming forms which when released, will swim off to find new fish hosts. White spot can be fatal if it severely damages the gills. Proprietary white spot medications are usually effective in dealing with the problem, especially combined with raising the temperature to around 28°C (82°F), which speeds up the life cycle so that the chemically more sensitive free swimming stages are exposed to the treatment. However, recurrence is common.

Other skin parasites

Large parasites such as fish lice (Argulus sp) are occasionally encountered. These are easily visible with the naked eye and can be removed by first dabbing the louse with alcohol (which anaesthetisies it and weakens its grip) and then removing with a pair of tweezers.

Pictured:
A beautiful and healthy
male Pearl gourami
(Trichogaster leerii)

This is best left to a veterinarian Fish that are scratching, rubbing, have a high breathing rate and/or patches of grey on the skin (excessive mucus production) are likely to have some microscopic parasitic problems. This can be one of several protozoal infestations or a fluke problem. Use a proprietary anti-protozoan medication.

Fungus

This classically looks like a cotton-wool patch stuck on to the fish, which collapses when the fish is taken from the water. Proprietary medications including malachite green, 2-phenoxyethanol or pimenta extract. Salt added to the water will often inhibit the growth of fungi, even down to 1 to 3 grams per litre. Many apparent fungal infections are actually parasitic, because the thick mucus that skin parasites trigger can form dense, fluffy patches on the skin surface.

Bacterial

Bacterial infections are common in ornamental fish. Typical symptoms include blood spots and ulcers. Some of these may respond to proprietary anti-bacterial medications containing tea tree extract or acriflavine. Some infections may require antibiotics. In most countries these are controlled drugs and are available only under the direction of a veterinarian. Certain infections, such as fish tuberculosis, are extremely difficult to cure and may require the fish to be euthanased.

Tumours

Fish, especially older ones, can develop tumours and growths. It can sometimes be possible for a veterinarian to operate and remove a growth, although this may depend upon a number of different factors including the size and location of the tumour.

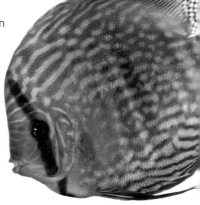

Volume of your tank

If you prefer your units in gallons, you can use this conversion chart:

Volume in litres	Volume in UK gallons	Volume in US gallons
1	0.2	0.3
2	0.4	0.5
5	1.1	1.3
10	2.2	2.6
20	4.4	5.3
30	6.6	7.9
40	8.8	10.6
50	10.9	13.2

Measurements rounded to 1 decimal place.